The sting of it

A.J. Odasso

Tolsun Books
Tolleson, Arizona & Las Vegas, Nevada

The Sting of It

Edited by David Pischke

Set in Mrs. Eaves OT, 12pt font.
Design by David Pischke

ISBN 978-1-948800-25-9

Published by Tolsun Books, LLC
Tolleson, Arizona & Las Vegas, Nevada
www.tolsunbooks.com

For all the friends who kept me alive
when I believed I was already gone

TABLE OF CONTENTS

Part I.

Part II.

ACKNOWLEDGEMENTS

"Push" and "Night Riding" first appeared in the March/April 2009 issue of BSFA's *Focus*

"Nightmares" first appeared under the title "Three Nightmares" in the Spring 2010 issue of *Illumen*

"What It Is" first appeared in Issue 3 of *Ouroboros Review*

"Moving Shakespeare's Bones" first appeared in Issue 157 *of Snakeskin*

"Fragment" and "Ivy" first appeared in Issue 4 of *The Battersea Review*

"Orbital" first appeared in Issue 13 of *Farrago's Wainscot*

"Persephone, Trapped" first appeared in Issue 35.1 of *Star*Line*

"Ink Archaeologist" first appeared in Issue 1 of *Through the Gate*

"Stone Ghost" first appeared in Issue 4 of *inkscrawl*

"The Book of Drowned Things" first appeared in *Strange Horizons*, 19 September 2011

"Returning Song" first appeared in *Strange Horizons*, 4 June 2012

"Fairy Beekeeper" first appeared in *Strange Horizons*, 31 December 2012

"The Archer's Daughter" first appeared in *Heavenly Bodies* from Beautiful Dragons Press

"Bone-House" first appeared in a slightly different form in Issue 4 of *Liminality*

"Transition Metal" first appeared in *My Dear Watson* from Beautiful Dragons Press

"Rigel" first appeared in Book (Issue) 4 of *Dark Mountain*

"The Calm Before," "Outbound," & "Oblivious" first appeared in *Belmont Story Review*, Spring 2016

"Red Wire," "Hunters," & "Slipknot" first appeared in Issue 17 of *SWAMP Writing*

"Your last word on earth" first appeared in Issue 38.2 of *Star*Line*

"XX / XY" first appeared in *Mythic Delirium*, June 2016

"Jellyfish" & "Out of Water" first appeared in Issue 8 of *Liminality*

"Sargasso Sea" first appeared in *Remixt: Volume 1*, September 2016

"Widening Gyre" first appeared in *Not a Drop* from Beautiful Dragons Press

"Nothing Goes Away" & "Ace of Spades" first appeared in *New England Review of Books*, November 2016

"Tenebrae" first appeared in *New England Review of Books*, March 2017

"Radiant Things" first appeared in *Noble Dissent* from Beautiful Dragons Press

"Hurricane Party" first appeared in Issue 3 of *Rascal Journal*

"Keepsake" first appeared in *Climbing Lightly Through Forests: An Ursula K. Le Guin Tribute Poetry Anthology* from Aqueduct Press

"Fireflies Gone," "Origin Story," "What It Is," "Undertow," "The Breakers Fail," and "Cruel Sister, Revised" first appeared in the *Turn RPG* book from Daedalum Analog Productions

You who do not remember
passage from the other world
I tell you I could speak again: whatever
returns from oblivion returns
to find a voice

Louise Glück, "The Wild Iris"

PART I

push

They say it works perfectly, this slab
made of stone that may be the only thing
between us and the darkness. Deftly,

lift your hand and sign grief, brush the sand
from your eyes, and know that eternity
is a pivot-swing and a single step

forward if you would but place your palms
against the blackness and pray for amends
to be made. You, standing there living

and breathing, know that this threshold sends
us to where the horses are running
and dragging us. We are here waiting

for death, for an answer, for the door—

Night Riding

The company of the dead have been riding
about in my sleep these past nights, asking
favors. "Will you buy me some envelopes—"

"—some paper? Some pins? And will you sing—"
"—for my daughter, my mother? Find my ring?"
I freeze by the windy roadside as they pass

in a clatter of hooves and cloaks and shoes
from all times and places, their many pale faces
drunk with dew and moonlight to behold me.

If I wake, I wonder, will the grass
be as green in the place where I stood
if I might find it? Or will I see

the cloaks and the horses, the midnight
gloom of the forest and the watch-fires
of the hunt's master and its sentinels,

who have no need of paper, pins, *or* sleep?

nightmares

I.

We're low in the hull as the floor's ripped open
ahead of us, black water gurgling inescapably up

through the carpet. My stocking feet get soaking
wet, but my only thoughts are for the picture, priceless,

and your birthday present inexplicably left on a shelf
in our cabin's small closet. I'm not sure how we arrive,

but I'm laughing all the way, making wise-cracks about *Titanic*,
which you don't find funny in the least, your voice urgent

as I dash from drawer to backpack and back again, gathering
the things that I feel are important. That you *can't*.

2.

Chez Mai has expanded since last
we were here, only we've never
been here before. I'm aghast

at the girl beside you at the table,

some painted whore of a time-traveler
from Moulin Rouge. You speak to her
gently, as if my disapproval might shatter

the only dream that you've found willing

and able.

3.

If only the backwoods were as quiet as these spaces
between us. You in your slumber, mumbling, reach for
my fingers cold and trembling. I wake while you snore on
in whatever teeth-grinding vision you have asked for.

what stays

Fold your arms and bow your head, they said,
so I obeyed. No matter, my heart,
if this means we've been betrayed. We'll find
a space in the earth that will be only
ours and slowly become through the passage
of time a grave. It is no hard thing
to lie in the sun for breaths out of mind
and then none. We will take some memory
from the stone, and give our blood in its place
so that our bones might not blow to dust.

Take hold of my hands now. You must.

moving shakespeare's bones

I set my hands upon the stone and left prints
in the dust—so thick you could have swept it
across the threshold and into oblivion.
We who honor dead men's words are wary
of curses, as if even that self-same act
were violation. What bits and motes be bone,
we cannot say. And as for the fabled stone,
it lies immune to coaxing—no adoration
in verse is sufficient to lift it, not even
the imprint of its master's voice. I'm able
to wait out this ageless recitation
for only so long. Where words fail to gentle,
I'll pry it until my fingers are bloodied
with care. Be moved, and I'll yet forebear.

undertow

The storm must have known
my slow-eyed waking was long

overdue: the sky stark, swollen
overhead with the knowledge

of my passing from dreams
into death. There are sparrows

caught in the chimney to this
very day, their shallow songs

echoing down the river
of years since I first spoke

of longing to fly. Thunder,
replace this faltering heart

with a clockwork swallow,
give me voice to wonder

at the love of the rain
for the brambles, pin-pricks

leaving my wrists in shambles
as I move between these worlds

that hope to have me. Two clicks
of my heels and I'm gone again,

off on a wing and a prayer,

or maybe

a dare.

KATADESMOS

1: for dismissing me as mere hearts and flowers

This is why

I lost too many before I learned. Listen
to what this aching has to tell you; grief
is not worth twice its length in tears
if the fulcrum fails to pitch. Observe
your repetition for what it obscures.

I've had enough of loss, sufficient shock
for these countless voices carried. So look
to the turn of your fingers on keys, to sheer
absence of sleep. Trawl the dark for day
and don't linger: once grasped, it fades.

I don't repair the broken lightly. Learn
that patches must be plied, stitches won
from shards lodged in far-too-eager arms.

Don't speak of softness to me. What peace
I grant these survivors, they've earned—

no heart but my hands be bloodied,
no bloom but my breath be burned.

2: for what you did to me and to the others

wall and wave

Come the end,
that line you toed
was laid so low—

ill-dreaming, they cost
breath; well-seeming,
love failed to amend

what lives we lost

to tide-lined concrete,
thoughtless wave, and
whisper-wrought belief

that their eyes, their hearts
and the sum of our parts
were not worth saving

for light—

I will ask you
one last time, fierce
enemy mine: what price
was worth this breaking?
How deep would you pitch
into forgetting

who we are?

ɤou'll ɴever ᴋɴow

I was the one to throw
the first stone. That shout
in the void was what we needed,
and so I fashioned a voice—for thoughts
are things my words can sow best, besides seeds
of subtle dissent. I watch friends wedge jagged pebbles
in the crack to assuage their grief. We watch strangers snap,
hear them plead with you, false deity, who won't listen or warn them
what horrors loom. My door is open to howling, welcomes unforgiving sea:
and the weary do come. We are stronger than you think, we whispers, and we
push with our backs, our hands splayed against the glass. Your edifice shudders.

ALL IT TAKES IS

One shard
of doubt
to bring
down
Babel:

we smile
and watch
the fabled
tower
fall

fragment

I'd leave the creepers as they are. Bless the casements
if they should crumble; there's more than time enough

to make repairs. English ivy and fierce-twining roses
on this shore or another would suit. Now, I will wish it

our corner here in the dreaming,
and write until it is so.

IVY

One fine morning, it's the ivy
that will show you: your bones
have all split at the seams. Arrows
are made easily from these. Learn
that nobody else has your back. Trust
is more often than not for the weak,
and love unforgivable. Your stone heart,
you must split in four; poison the quarters
with marrow from each shaft. It'll hurt
no greater than what wounds you have.
Always watch the ivy. Study both cracks
and rebinding. Nock swiftly now, aim quick
to court the kill. Your tendril-bound breath
fills each fissure like ivy. Now, *watch*.

orbital

Once, before there was
your voice, I wrote lies

just as I am lying
to you now.

I seek cause-bound
effect, action with
sound consequence
in the trajectory
arc of your text.

There is none of my truth
so deeply entrenched here
that you will not find it:

the secret is less to solve
for these variables hidden
than what you must guess.

There is how the pyre
was prepared for us,

there is how the fire
made lovers of us—

what I want and
who you are
is one and
the same.

Now that there is your voice,
my lies bend to intersect.

Your breath solves
for the sound
of my name.

persephone, trapped

It'll be a good deal for you, they said, feigning pity
as they stamped the official-looking document
without my consent. You would think that deities' rights
would have meant something here, but not lately.

Even now, I fail to grasp why this is different:
I haven't missed a mortal body, not one bit.

This model easily breaks. It feels imaginary pain
at the slightest written provocation. It weeps
to hear strains so many pale shades short
of Orpheus's lyre. It takes no certain joy
in fleshly pleasures, only burns when verse
is sunk like an axe-blade in its veins.

There's sweetness, though, that's unexpected—
the fiery shiver in her quiet eyes when he comes
in the door, the fervent longing to touch him
even though she doesn't. She waits for him to make
the first move, and her welcome is as cool
as grape-skin ready to yield. Her grandfather's garden
was Eden, and she struggles to express the taste
of sugar-pears in one soft, restrained brush
of her lips. She remembers pain yet undetected.

And then there are my eyes, the fractured yielding
of the mirror as I numbly realize that their color
has changed. Where once they were unfaltering gray,
these irises feather and splinter with shades
of sheer yearning. Blue, silver. Fey-wild burning
like a storm-tossed, wreck-riddled sea. Still hungry.

No different, I tell them.
Not one bit.

ink archaeologist

Already they itch, fresh rifts in my skin:
glyphs carved by needle are not wounds,
but excavation: shoulder blade, hip-bone,
and forearms signposted. My first lover
traced words on my back in darkness; now
this lone feather, quill for a god & witch-wand
to his wife, bears stark witness. My friend
of many years, best-beloved, once marked
the spot where *forever* becomes my flesh.
The man who has coaxed other treasures
over heart-line, nerve-shine, deep-hidden veins
had eyes as old as the hands that once shaped
these sigils to life. His gentle tongue wove
spells as he worked, so fondly revered them.

stone ghost

Ancient monster, I remember the day
I first saw your face, spread my fingers

on the glass and breathed in awe. Eyeless,

your ghost peered through text and reflection
to welcome me home: *This was the sea,*

my daughter. Your time has come.

what it is

The town's what it is because they're in it,
because of the blueberries in the brush
that my grandfather planted one summer
before they took the fox and shot the thrush,
which ate my grandmother's jam-making crop
off the brambles, because night on Summit
Street seethes with firefly-streaks above the drop

down to where my father swam the river
while they tamed the fox and named it
Lady, my uncle played jazz and shot pool
down the ditch that almost had his brother
when a deer crossed his path in the splendor
of the half-moon on my mother's white face,
the babe she caught that night on the water

because the town's what it is, what we are.

Fairy Beekeeper
for Silvia Gasparini

You teach me patience, send jars of sunlight
that require careful straining. Your children

spin gold from acacia and rose, turn blood shades
into caring sweetness. You did not know me

from either inhabitant of Eden, but still you threw
wide your garden gates and said: *Come, taste*.

Whence I've come in such condition—my wings
in shreds, hum broken—you took the time to ask.

Now, I take my tea with a fine skim of wax.

the Book of Drowned Things

The man in the wine shop gives me half a glass
of sweet French red, tells me it's been popular
at weddings. He blithely calls it port, but I can't
help but think: *It's madeira in a stained pink dress.*
I carry one slim bottle beneath my arm just as far
as the spirits section at the back. I confess
it's a share of Guyana rum that I'm really after.
Fifteen-year aged in an oak cask is the stuff
on which my dreams are made and broken,
unless you count the time, five vodka shots
and several tons of knife-edged heartbreak later,
I locked myself in Brian and Jody's loo and shouted
at an imaginary dead boy for half an hour. It's true
that I'm built for heartbreak, and so I raise
this toast to friends loved, lost, and about
to be lost. Death has always wanted me closer
than those she steals from my arms. It's you
that I can never hope to save, and so I'll tell
this story before I forget: as a child, I drowned
off North Carolina. I remember the crush of water
in my lungs and the vicious sting of salt
all the sun-shot way down. I remember the calm
that stole over me less than half a minute before
I hit the sand and choked up her gifts to me, grief
before glory. *You're the ferryman now,* she said.

And, fool that I am, I believed it.

Returning Song
on reading "Derek Jarman's Garden"

Speak to me, friend, long dead
though you are. Tell me of home
there by the sea, of how salt
killed the kale, but spared
the dog-rose. Red Admirals came
to you as they now come to me:
winged and fearless, never far
from our upturned palms.

We suffer a fever, some say,
of tragic proportions. Our sin
is the folly of Sappho, the grief
of Alexander. We are cousin
to mischief, you and I,
my departed brother. You gift
this world with thorny warp
and root-ridden weft.

The quiet house, my still heart,
your books on the table.

It is as if I never left.

suspension

Time and again, you ask me if I believe in spirits,
in phenomena that can't be measured. I remember
halting on the bridge, staring out across the water,
unable to answer. I've seen strange things. There are bits
of one place or another hanging about where they don't
belong. I've seen a man die and leave behind him a space
in the world that was not there before and another man
rise to fill it with chilling grace. I've seen everything
that my parents prayed I never would. I'm granted grace
too good for me and far beyond my years. There is music
in that corner that should have faded with my tears. It won't,
I'm certain, not ever. And if I were to return to that moment
on the bridge, where we stood staring long into the distance,
I'd find myself murmuring—*Yes, but just for one instant.*

The Archer's Daughter

These long years now, insatiable, I have craved
Anacardiaceae. Cashews on relatives' coffee tables
crushed between my milk teeth, dried mangoes at
nineteen, tried for the first time, wolfed wisely down.
My grandmother noticed uninterrupted flesh day in

and day out during interminable summers I spent
neck-deep in feral creepers: leaf, limb, and branch
caught fierce in my rose-lit hair. That day, I was two,
had gone crawling fearless into bluets, then brush—

intractable dirt dug with slight pliant fingers, yearning
for earth. I'd gone straight to root, heart, and nerve
of poisoned arrow. From the greens she pulled me,

she, unbeknownst to my ravening blood
and bated breath, also immune.

Bone-House

Your tongue wounds me still,
your words sunk thorn-sharp
in my marrow. You're a vice
I never gave up, no matter

what I may claim when my lover
pries. *Hús-bónd*, house-bound
to blood and bone my heart
has been, but not to home.

Your eyes, bright-weft, my brick
and mortar, your quick mind
my only thrill.

Handle with care

Needles, green. There's pine-sharp light
on this dove-feathered morning. Breeze
past rust-screened window, off leaves—

my mother's strayed dawn-wise roving
through bright trees. As for my father,
no-one knows where he sleeps. I shiver

to cousins' dismay. Witch-child, hellion,
so-young-she-speaks, *Where has Mom gone?*
They marvel there's none so quiet as me

in my grief. *Orphaned early*, I think, but lack
enough breath to seethe. Word-wild, fearful,
slip cabin-latch and cinderblock. The breach

is old-wood, is shadow, is dust. Beyond it—
brave voices, bruised sea.

Transition Metal

I learned metals early. My uncle,
a jeweler, garlanded his mother

in gold. My grandmother's rings
held diamond, topaz, and garnet

too costly for words. At nine,
she fitted a circlet, silver, set

with blood-flecked carbon
on my little finger. I grew

till I had to thread it through
that cheap herringbone chain

a hopeful beau gave me. Kiss
girls after sundown and no-one

will see you wear moonlight
where others insist you don sun.

Rigel
for Jane Yolen

I was fresh home from naming quasars
the night we first met, your silk-soft paws
pressed flush to my palms. Your eyes
were mismatched: one the color of bluets
stripped back; the other, new spring grass.

My grandfather taught me to hunt. He said
you'd prove a rabbit-chaser's friend, but my heart
and yours, dear girl, were set on a different prize—
dusk-wise, we wandered those rocky hillsides
in search of blue stars. You trained so swift
to the slightest turn of my hand, read warning
in the faintest puff of my wondering breath.

I'm glad now that I knew you in winter,
wolf-sister. Your first daughter would have run
with me had you not gone, might've greeted Orion
as a seasoned old friend. As I still do, my sweet,
and as I dream. As roaming we always did.

PART II

red wire

Boston Common, 2013. The test
results arrive. Internet geneticists
have decoded my fragility. Blink
at the likelihood of psoriasis. Hold
breath as BRCA1 & 2 show clear,
but say: *Other mutations may exist.*

Time bomb, this body, weeded already
of cysts, endometrium, womb. My chest
fills with doubt, knowing what comes next
will always be the question. My thoughts
turn to introspection: *The parts I want
least are poison-coded in my genes.*

Bleeding, I do not miss. Benign aberrations
are far behind me now. What I must hide
concerns prescience of danger: *My last wish
is the one extraction most likely to be denied.*

The calm before

Evening primrose, bittersweet. This city's wish
is to stand long after we've left it. Drowsy green
will swallow our stories and crush them
to seeding. Ley-line and trestle-bridge alike
know our full stops, caesuras, palimpsests
before we've but breathed them. Our smoke
in the evening swan-wake shimmers patient
as frost. The next harsh winter stands waiting
already. Poison ivy reaches, tendriled warning
against restless belief. Yes, you will leave me
alone here in undisguised autumn. Your hands,
I trust less than this toxin-shine, your berry-rime
on my baited lips, so let me be. There's still time.

Hobbyist

I find the florist's cacti intractable, walk in
off the street. My habit of photographing

rose petals scattered across filthy tile, snow-slushed
brick, and leaf-littered concrete beckons. The guy

at the counter says he doesn't mind when I ask him,
thumb already on digital shutter, if I can snap a few.

I buy cuttings for his trouble. I do not think of you.

outbound

Trackside again,
spellbound. I remember the drowned
girl, the haunted tower. Roving lakeside

here in the snow is how we courted. The stars
would brook neither of us, and you would not

harbor me. Dear heart of my undoing,
for you I'd have braved the spring.
Would've stayed.

oblivious

It's your hair that tempts me first—
red ash and chestnut. *What a catch*

you must have been, I think, dizzied
by the speed at which you blink

behind lenses in well-thumbed frames.
The quirk of your mouth comes next,

that insatiable tilt in lieu of a smile
as you skirt my gaze. It's your hands

I get hung up on—thin digits, tensile
wrists. Your knuckles clamp book-spines

as you maunder, tautly halting my eye
at the half-round band on your finger.

Hunters

Your progress through six months of poison
begins. Three days in, you have migraines
to beat the band; three weeks on, your hair
is almost gone. How fast our cells slip

through sheerest trauma is the catch
to our warp and weft. Surgeons say
my healing's too swift; oncologists

prod at your lymph nodes' refusal
to rest. What monsters we are,
mother, remains to be seen—

in the end, what is a wound
but a door through which
blood leaves?

Dinner with Janet Echelman's
As if it were Already Here

The wind tilts her
my way. We decide
to have dinner, agree

that Nebo looks fittest
for netting and flesh. I order
Sanpellegrino the precise color
of her current lower-right edge.

I ask her how it's been out here, with
shades of the sea and tall ships below her
in tea-stained memory of salt. She shudders
bellows-like, resplendence of spring green
and iris, voiceless semblance of laughter.

I offer her a taste of pomodoro,
but she declines. I ask her if,
chameleon-like, she eats
of the air. I map her

against latticed sky,
unspooling regret—
or shared hunger.

The Devil in Boston
after Leonard Cohen's "Satan in Westmount"

Here, *he* becomes *she*—
or neither. Both, all
shades between, cannily suit.
Satan strolls Charles Street
in motorcycle boots, denim,
      and flannel, fresh
      from a weekend
      in Maine. Sips pumpkin spice,
      clove-starved, insatiable;
trades those hummed Spanish
lays chased by Dante's tercets
for Decemberists lyrics, although
the aptly manicured fingernails
remain. As for the asphodel,
there's a softer lapel in which
      to put it. *My regrets,*
      this sprig says,
      follow you to the grave.

fireflies gone

My grandmother wrapped me in rouge
one cacophonous October, told me
my father had worn the same dress.

Tomboyish as Red, I asked if she wished Dad
had been a girl. She said, "Don't worry
what I wished for, my sweet." I went

to a Halloween party that night and danced
with goblins, ghosts, hoodlums, boys in sheets.
After, I couldn't find my fleece-lined shoes

in the darkness, in the brush. Duck, duck, *wolf.*

slipknot

Boston Common, 2015. The PCP-ordered test
comes back conclusive. Medical geneticists
have documented my alterity. BRCA variants
still absent, but another mutation does exist:
CHEK2 is what I carry, and it
harbors a risk too high.

Blink at sheer likelihood of that lump
returning, at the knowledge of alleles
gone awry. Time bomb, this ribcage
strained with doubt. What comes next
is the weight I must ferry. My chest
comprises the ever-unwanted sum
of my parts: *This extraction*
a debt as-yet unpaid.

Bleeding, I will not miss once
the cutting is finished. Absence
of benign aberration abounds: *Denied*
safe passage, grant my fiercest wish.

nothing goes away

"If there's anything we know about the autistic brain,"
states Dr. Wolf, watching me, intent, "it's that nothing
goes away." In answer—cautious, but content—I nod,
consider what to say. I would like to tell her my mind
is a shattered mirror, that its prodigal fragments scatter
to every last crevice and corner, beyond tenable hope
of retrieval. Simulacra ensnared, writhing, relivable,
freed from their original frames. Longing to confess
that glass—cold-to-molten, mercury-backed—transforms
thought into pierced flesh soundly refuses translation,
slips my tongue. Thank the keyboard gods for pristine
conveyance, but a pen's what I'm stuck with. My wrist
jerks stiffly; my fingers jot cliffs. *Once I'm home*, I think,
I'll get this down, fashion you verse of it. And then I blink.

DNR

I am so thin, reads the mimeograph, final line
in my great-grandmother's letter. Records say
it was consumption that killed her, slow wasting-
away of hunger and breath. *I am so thin*, she says
again, her last graphite-scrawl a repetition.

•

I have known fever, fire gone viral in my blood
after swift incubation. H1N1-haunted dreams
raised my temp to a hundred and three. I lay
raving for days while the NHS Direct hotline
told my partner to keep me warm. *I think I'm
dying*, I rasped, grabbing the phone. *I'm afraid.*

•

Clean typeface in lieu of scrawling, nib-fine
ascenders scaffold a loved-one's living will.
Do not resuscitate, it says, deceptively brief
with dotted *I* and curtly-crossed *T*s. *We are so
thin*, I think, signing the paper. *We are so thin.*

Haunting Harvard Square

Grief grow gaunt, and breath
blow still. Leaves, new brightness
in the shivering, silvering green
are all I can ask. Stay a while
with me here if you can. Let's pass
from rusted lock to riverbed
under cloud-bled blue: no chance
will steer us from the path
on which we're set. One heel
ahead of the other, your ghost
just a step behind. Red Line
to the right of us, Charles tide-
line to the left. Only you
know where we're going,
fierce-footed even in death.

Timepiece

You put your watch—
worn, Timex, cheap—
in my hand. I was nine.
You said, "Listen,
those oil drums behind
the garage are about
to blow." The coil of
my digits unwound.
I was nine. You said,
"Lit trash fell out-
side the burn barrel.
The oil will catch.
Get your brother
and your sisters
in the car." I was
nine. And you said,
"I'm going back. I'll
try to put it out. Get
the kids in the car
and drive if I don't
come back." But Dad,
you did. Every word,
each tick. We lived.

Treasure

Silk from a sow's ear,
you called me once—

No Miss America,
but smart as fuck.

Three pretty sisters
obscured my looks.

The middle pair, you loved
passing well. The youngest,

you touched like chattel
while she fixed her hair.

Silk from a sow's ear,
you called me once.

My mouth spills coins,
a hangman's purse.

prosthetics

We put on dresses Sunday morning,
our private joke. Old friends will
want to see us at church. Mom says
it's really nice to have us home.

I know the nearness now
of death, and your brave face
feels like a punch-line. We sit
through Sacrament still as saints.

After bread and water, after talks
that set my Jewish teeth on edge
and you to drawing on your arm,
we endure handshakes. Glassy

smiles reflect what I know
better than to suspect: all eyes
low, lashes frown. We flee
before Second Hour sends

invitations to scripture study
our way. We take Mom's car,
zip to Sheetz, order hot dogs
with chili, onion, and cheese.

Some drops right on my chest.
You laugh, say there's nothing
left to catch it. I think about
those pious, lowered eyes

and puzzled smiles. You say
you remember the location
of that creepy cabin filled
with dozens of fake arms

and ancient newsprint. I say
I'd like to see it. You drive
through drizzle a little while
till the dirt road rises. Gladly

I'd have struck out through trees
to hunt this slumber-party legend,
but we stare through the fog-slick
windshield. My twin scars ache.

Maybe next time we'll try
trespassing, you say. I nod,
chewing in silence. We go on,
watching for deer in the rain.

cruel sister, revised

after several Child Ballads

No undead harp for stringing:
neither you, nor I. My heart
has ferried yours these five
and twenty years gone

so the river cannot
claim us. The miller's
daughter becomes me:
swan-kind, blue-garbed

instead. The red, you see,
is in my hair. None ever
sang she had a sister, too,
but discord is the music's

undoing: cry murder; cry
false, false! The truest
have you been of all fair
yarrow, darling child, but

our once-upon-a-times burn
contrariwise: mercy isn't for
the likes of love unspoiled.
The breastbone harp lies.

Jellyfish

June 2004

This month's attack is
fierce without the pill,

shot-through innards
in shallow hot water

find no relief. I splay
once-curled fingers, slick

belly becoming
licked wound: no touch

sufficient to stay
the tendrils at point

of tangling, no pool
saline enough

to soothe sting
from null seed.

XX / XY

Londoners, Midlanders all. The helix
has yielded this seed. No need to ask

for your blood, no need to test beyond
your so-called daughters. Carry this,

and we carry both threads. Accident
has tangled this recessive. Undress me

again and ask: at what price freedom
from the sensation of grit-fine glass

when I swallow because toxic drip
has conquered my tongue? Mother,

these twin monsters
have already won.

sargasso sea

I.

scylla
July 2001 – September 2005

It's always tough. My first
two lovers, a man and then

a woman, noticed. No room
on penetration, no harbor

from storm. Grin and bear it
is what I learned: to bleed

every time. Fresh wound
unrelenting, but pain

I devour. Riddle thrust
in me. Hard rain.

2.

charybdis
November 2005

My third lover
arrives. *You look*

a little different down
there, he says. Imagine

me falling, imagine me near

the whirlpool's edge. *Inside, too,*
I answer. *Inside, monstrous. Can*

you hear it? Siren-song
follows. I cave in.

3.

shipwreck
December 2012

Enough discomfort

is enough. I choose to
go under the knife. Skin

in excess, shorn down; canal

below the accepted limit
observed. *You might*

want to look into it.

4.

salvage
November 2014

Back under. All spoils
but wayward gonads
plundered. Cervix
untethered, that
ungainly hatch.

Cyst-filled tubes
clipped to the quick.

*Uterus specimen smaller
than expected.* You'd

never have borne it.

5.

sρoils
December 2015 – July 2016

Mutation. Prow, too,
disproportionate risk.

Undertow, lead
me through ether

a third-charmed
time. Whisper,

*He'd never
have stayed
to tread in
your wake.*

Prescient hindsight
unwinds. Buoyant,

I swim free of it.

widening gyre

I think of the way I sank that rosy granite stone
shaped like a heart in the duck-pond shallows
because when you plucked it up from the floor

of Merlin's Cave at low tide while incense burned
I decided there was no way in hell that I would go
back to the kind of existence in which passports

might dictate the hour minute day even second
of our end on that craggy beach with sunset
your halo and porphyry my last-wish relic

I think of the way I sank that stone
shaped like a heart in the shallows

I think of the way I sank
in the shallows shaped

like a heart

out of water

In my dream,
the dead girl
lay unfound
for hours
on the floor,

three blankets
heaped on her
while the others
tussled, drank,
and whispered

till dawn. Face
pale, her eyes
clear, haunted
out of living
to meet mine.

.

I woke at ten,
turned on
the lights, sick
with the sight
of this fiction.

Scraped dust
from my toes,
noted clean
floorboards
beneath.

Collapsed
back against
percale sheets,
unraveled,
done. Slept

an hour and
a half, maybe
more. Woke
eleven-thirty
to wet sounds,

panic. Switch hit,
feet bare: two fish
have escaped
the tank. One dry,
long gone; one

gasping for air,
pearly skin livid.
She waited there
next to my shoes,
gills and eyes clear.

equinox

for my great-aunt

It was the jawbone in the grass
that told me. Bad enough the house
was empty, sad enough the spot
was where you'd buried the dog.
Veteran trespasser have I been
all these years, only half blood
to these women I've loved—no,
even that secret you will not take
to the grave. My trade is knowing
what others guess; my grandmother
survives you and will leave these teeth
in my bleach-stripped hands long after
goldenrod and bramble weave over
dormant moss. My crime is to recall
what you have been in this corner
of the moonflower-planted world
I roamed and roam still. Your loss
is a sister yet breathing, my grief
a recounting scattered on the hill.

Things Being What They Are

Maybe it starts with
my great-grandmother
in the orchard
meeting her lover,
for all stories
of this kind start
with a woman
and a tree
and a man.

I might mention
the rot underfoot
is from pears
instead of apples,
that the bush
behind which
they hide yields
berries blue
as night sky.

When they're
found out,
she's already
with child.

My unborn grandmother's
grandmother kicks him
out. Tells her daughter,
"You can't marry
some foreigner,"
where the phrase

some foreigner
equals
that Jew.

Maybe it proceeds with
my great-grandmother
married off quick
to the other suitor,
with my grandmother's
younger sister
never knowing
the truth.

There's a whisper
in our history,
so we ask,
"Who?"

"Some foreigner,"
says my grandmother's
cousin, nine decades
on, revealing
a name. That Jew
is what I discover,
tracing pear-seeds
back through.

Orchard
equals
our blood,
the gene

that led to
the illness
that led to
the test.

It ends with
my grandmother,
in her nineties,
picking regrets.

It starts with
me, determined
to climb, to gather
the rest.

magdalena, NM

for my father

This is a real cowboy town, you say, driving us
off Alamo Navajo Reservation, scanning sky
and Sandias through the windshield for miles.
The dental clinic's behind us. My jaw's shot
to hell, all those glass vials, seven Marcaine
and three Lidocaine down—enough to kill
a child. Maybe that's why your mind's set
on target practice somewhere unregulated.
Like they do out here, you explain, shotgun
in the trunk. I barely respond, stuck on signs
for motels and RV parks sand-scraped with age.
I find a bone in the ruins of Kelly Ghost Town
three miles out—vertebral, arcane. Bullets echo
in the unearthly quiet, stillness unbroken between
except for the breeze. *I fell in love with this place*,
you tell me once we're back on the road. I think,
eleven years on from when you moved, I've fallen,
too, but those voices I hear in the rasp of yellow
sage aren't the same as yours. With each trigger-pull,
I saw apparitions fraught against all that wild blue—

Datura trumpets, stiffly triumphant, faded too soon.

The Recto Fragments

FOR SALE: Two pages from a French prayer-book, ca. 1420

folio 31

Draw me in, blue-veiled beauty. Your tears
singe my skin: this heart can feel again

in spite of the dust that confounds me.
I've been sick to death's brink, senses dulled

by the promise of wellness. It takes years,
so turn the page / set the clock / halt the spell

of ink-blot poison in my veins. His skin
a tracery of rust-tracks and thorn, his ears

deaf shells a-ring with mourning. His eyes.

Yours.

folio 180

Did you not die already?

I saw—
the shroud, the tomb. The wounds
unburdened of blood. Wings

in the webbing
of your hair. Your mother
made round, low sounds

like a *[quill-scraped]* bird

or—

a *[salt-stained]* fish. Shrubs
in the distance. Barrow-mounds
of sand, the Dead Sea.

Your drying wish.

Hers.

Radiant Things

for Emma Goldman

You, too, were a wayward daughter, refused
to bend beneath your father's lash. You, too,
made a so-called bad bride—five dollars
in hand, you left that jealous bastard
behind. No mother would you prove; no
mother, I. New York gave you lovers,
spindle and thread, a pulpit from which
to throw sparks. You whipped your mentor
when he betrayed you, perhaps incited
assassination at thirty-two. What I
wouldn't give to have been as brave, to put
bullets behind my words. You, too, lost
what you thought you loved most—this time,
Emma, I see it. We, too, are Mother Earth.

Regent's Park Honey

First taste of London in months,
ivy-bite and sun. Rose nectar

a pallid backdrop, dormant
as hellebore musk. My grief

dissolves; crystalline doubt
begs peace no more. This

is your war I've walked into
unaware, my clipped tongue

eager. Swallowed, undone.

At Victoria Station

For God's sake, you said, squeezing my shoulders, *I'll do
better keeping in touch*. From your arms to ticket barrier,

I swayed—unheld, alone once you slipped out-of-frame.
Since, I've taken shots to nerve and bone, nightshade

to numb what I did not dream. Doubtful clamor shunts
these words of mine from ringing mind to page: *Won't let*

you forget, darling, what you've wrought. This horror, these
eyelids pinned wide. Read my world as I see it. Emptied

of meaning, save the spaces in between. What I think is
outstretched here in the quiet. Don't you dare blink.

Your last word on earth

might be my name, but it's hard to tell
through the prism of retraction. We sent

satellites forward in time at the speed
of thought; I need to know if I find you

again in the static, lest these glass bones
mis-refract. Message: *All that you love*

is enclosed in unforgiving stone. Response:
Then I will inter these shards, great city,

with your unrelenting ghost.

faithless

She has bad teeth, your ex-friend says. Small hands,
average build. Your latest French girl makes me look

like a model. Me: 5'3", crocus eyes, copper hair,
chest razed flat thanks to how the test came back.

I'm just not attracted to men, you said
to my face. *Just not attracted to men.*

I'd sink my white teeth in your neck,
watch you bleed for the sin of it.

I'd tell her to run given half a chance.

ace of spades

Trillium thrive on the strip-
mined hills, sip acid rain
like Prosecco. They wait
for love, or they make do
with sun. Underground
coal fires set tepid shoots
to yawning. Even roots
curled in thawing clay
know to wake. Split
the shale of my heart
for this last white-petaled
devotion. Rust streaks each
of three. Pick a card. Any.

The Devil Looks Different in Albuquerque

for Leonard Cohen, again

A genderfluid hipster Satan
is the only kind I ever saw
in Boston, but I'm still afraid.

I traded motorcycle boots (as much
of a chameleon act as I could manage)
for a pair of cowboy heels

with winged skulls
when I moved out here—
as you passed, I prayed

Shehecheyanu for days,
walked Central Avenue
in the unrelenting shade.

No desert creature,
your death pains me
more than I can say.

Let us look at your devil again.

origin story

Each death
a mirror:

teeth shed,
skin torn.

Each fin
an eddy:

etched,
unshorn.

Monster,
you call me.

I swim
farther

from shore.

The Breakers Fail

Cyclone-sighted,
cataclysmic:

my gaze, you said,
summoned storms

on the Atlantic.
Leviathan land-

locked, whirlpool
in human skin.

One year gone,
the day I tore

your net. Desert-
brash, my scales

glint with plunder
I clawed back.

You fade iron-
haired, tide-choked

for monstrous lack.

tenebrae

Pesach again.   Fresh fever, petal-strewn,

poulticed with ash.   With each extinguishing,

wish your steadfast way   into spring. Listen

to the echo now: strings   bowed, worn stone

longing to bend. The fault   in this blooming

is not your heart. Let the heavy   sky looming

take revenge if you cannot will it.   Tender any

glint of mercy you find needful: cleave   softly

to hope. Breathe wonder, find light upon leaving.

keepsake

Writing on the body, always
writing on the body, always
stories on bodies I am fighting
to keep alive, fictional bodies,
real bodies, *my body*; bodies
betrayed by their stories, *always*,
bodies in broken fictions
and in realities where they don't
belong, words and pictures needled ink-
scrawled blood-blurred *scarred*; if only
I could keep them safe, if only
I could keep them from ruin, if only
I could keep you, *if only*.

aftermath

I see us, fragile, as from a distance—
ephemera of nerve and bone. So much breath
contained in one cage, we explode.

I was not always afraid to speak my mind.
I was not always this shaking, mercurial knot
of pain. I, too, had vision. Lacked shame.

We cannot restore what our earliest days
erase. We reach for each other, think harder
on what we must say. Still, the tongue lashes.

The sting of it gives us away.

Hurricane party

There's been lightning these three nights, spark-dust
from the gathering clouds. I can't explain

why you don't haunt my dreams, why my heart's still
in the hull of my chest. When Death calls

these days, I can't answer for anguish
of still not belonging. Once, she wanted me

close, vaulted me breathing into the storm.
And breathing, breathing still, I'm alone

in the desert now. Flash-flood or hurricane,
find me. I'll drink to your coming.

Bear it, she pleads. *Breathe for me.*

A.J. Odasso's poetry has appeared in a variety of publications, including *Sybil's Garage, Mythic Delirium, Midnight Echo, Not One of Us, Dreams & Nightmares, Goblin Fruit, Strange Horizons, Stone Telling, Farrago's Wainscot, Liminality, Battersea Review, Barking Sycamores, SWAMP Writing, Belmont Story Review, New England Review of Books*, and *Rascal*. A.J.'s début collection, *Lost Books* (Flipped Eye Publishing), was nominated for the 2010 London New Poetry Award and was also a finalist for the 2010/2011 People's Book Prize. Their second collection with Flipped Eye, The *Dishonesty of Dreams*, was released in 2014; their third-collection manuscript, *Things Being What They Are*, an earlier version of *The Sting of It*, was shortlisted for the 2017 Sexton Prize. Their prose has appeared in the *Hidden Youth* (Crossed Genres) and *Knowing Why* (Autistic Self-Advocacy Network) anthologies, as well as in the Winter 2017 and Spring 2018 issues of *Pulp Literature*. They hold an M.F.A. in Creative Writing from Boston University and serve as Senior Poetry Editor at Strange Horizons magazine (www.strangehorizons.com)